How To Make The Dream God Gave You Come True

Kenneth Hagin Jr.

Unless otherwise indicated, all Scripture quotations in this volume are from the *King James Version* of the Bible.

First Printing 1981

ISBN 0-89276-708-1

In the U.S. write:
Kenneth Hagin Ministries, Inc.
P.O. Box 50126
Tulsa, Oklahoma 74150

In Canada write:
Kenneth Hagin Ministries
P.O. Box 335
Islington (Toronto), Ontario
Canada, M9A 4X3

BOOKS BY KENNETH E. HAGIN

Redeemed From Poverty . . . Sickness . . . Death
What Faith Is
Seven Vital Steps To Receiving The Holy Spirit
Right and Wrong Thinking
Prayer Secrets
Authority of the Believer
How To Turn Your Faith Loose
The Key to Scriptural Healing
The Ministry of a Prophet
The Origin and Operation of Demons
Demons and How to Deal With Them
Ministering to the Oppressed
Praying To Get Results
The Present Day Ministry of Jesus Christ
The Gift of Prophecy
Healing Belongs to Us
The Real Faith
The Interceding Christian
How You Can Know the Will of God
Man on Three Dimensions
The Human Spirit
Turning Hopeless Situations Around
Faith Food for Autumn
Faith Food for Winter
Faith Food for Spring
Faith Food for Summer
The New Birth
Why Tongues?
In Him
God's Medicine
You Can Have What You Say
How To Write Your Own Ticket With God
Don't Blame God
Words
Plead Your Case
How To Keep Your Healing
Laying on of Hands
A Better Covenant

Having Faith in Your Faith
Five Hindrances to Growth in Grace
Why Do People Fall Under the Power?
The Bible Way To Receive the Holy Spirit
I Believe In Visions
Exceedingly Growing Faith
The Woman Question
New Thresholds of Faith
Prevailing Prayer to Peace
Concerning Spiritual Gifts
Bible Faith Study Course
Bible Prayer Study Course
The Holy Spirit and His Gifts
Growing Up, Spiritually
Redimido De La Pobreza, La Enfermedad, La Muerte
La Fe, Lo Que Es
Siete Pasos Para Recibir El Espiritu Santo
?Piensa Usted Bien? O Mal?
La Autoridad Del Creyente
Como Desatar Su Fe
Seven Things You Should Know About Divine Healing
El Shaddai
Zoe: The God-Kind of Life
A Commonsense Guide to Fasting
How You Can Be Led By The Spirit of God
What To Do When Faith Seems Weak and Victory Lost
The Name of Jesus
The Art of Intercession

BOOKS BY KENNETH HAGIN JR.

Man's Impossibility—God's Possibility
Because of Jesus
UNITY: Key to the Age of Power
Faith Worketh by Love
Blueprint for Building Strong Faith
Seven Hindrances to Healing
The Past Tense of God's Word
Healing: A Forever-Settled Subject
How To Make the Dream God Gave You Come True

Contents

1. "Behold, the Dreamer!" 1

2. God Gave Me a Dream 5

3. Dare To Believe Your Dream 8

4. 13 Boys with a Vision 11

5. The Church's Vision:
   The World 15

6. A Word to Ministers 18

7. Quit Comparing 23

For the vision is yet for an appointed time,
but at the end it shall speak, and not lie:
though it tarry, wait for it;
because it will surely come,
it will not tarry.

—Habakkuk 2:3

Chapter 1
"Behold, the Dreamer!"

And they said one to another, Behold, this dreamer cometh.

—Genesis 37:19

"Behold, this dreamer cometh . . . ." These words were spoken about a man by the name of Joseph. His brothers said it.

Such words could be spoken of many people. You've probably heard them spoken in contempt of somebody who is always building "castles in the air" but never accomplishing anything. Such a person becomes known as a "dreamer."

However, these same words can be spoken respectfully of an individual who dreams a dream and makes that dream come true. Before, there was contempt: "Behold, the dreamer cometh." Now the same words are spoken with excitement: "Behold, the dreamer cometh!"

Let's look at the story of Joseph and his dream. One night he dreamed about shocks of wheat (representing his brothers) all bowing to one particular shock (representing him). Later, when he shared this dream with his brothers, they were skeptical and disgusted. They were jealous of Joseph. He was the youngest son and their daddy's "pet."

One day their father, Jacob, sent Joseph to see how his brothers and their flocks were doing. When the older brothers saw Joseph approaching, they looked at one another and said, "Hey, here comes the dreamer!"

They were still upset about his dream. When he

arrived at their camp, they grabbed him, threw him into an empty pit, and sold him to a passing caravan which was bound for Egypt. They said, "We're going to do away with this fellow and this dream he had of our bowing to him!"

The dream Joseph had was a dream from God, however. It was God's dream; not something Joseph had concocted. God had given the dream or vision to Joseph, as He has to others through the ages.

> **ACTS 2:17,18**
> **17 And it shall come to pass in the last days, saith God, I will pour out of my Spirit upon all flesh: and your sons and your daughters shall prophesy, and your young men shall see visions, and your old men shall dream dreams:**
> **18 And on my servants and on my handmaidens I will pour out in those days of my Spirit; and they shall prophesy.**

God has spoken to every one of us at some time in our life. He's given us dreams — He's given us visions — He's given us things to accomplish for Him. We're either involved with God's dream for us; we're letting it lie dormant; or we may be somewhere in the middle — lukewarm — working with it sometimes.

In this message I want to inspire you to get a new hold on your dream. Pull it off the shelf, dust it off, and get on with it.

Many of you feel trapped in failure, distress, or sickness. You must begin to dream in line with God's Word. You must see yourself a success. You must see yourself healed. You must see yourself more than a conqueror in Christ Jesus. You must see yourself greater than the circumstances around you, for *"greater is he that is in you, than he that is in the world"* (1 John 4:4).

Dare to dream big dreams for God! Purpose in your heart that the dream God has given to you will not lie dormant, but you will do something about it. You will accomplish it. You will succeed for Him.

No, I'm not talking about everybody rushing out and starting to travel, teach, and preach all over the world. I'm talking about doing what God has asked you to do in your own backyard — in your local church or fellowship — and then going on from that point.

Many people say, "In this highly mechanized and educated age, I can't do anything. I know God spoke to me, but I just don't see how it is possible to fulfill *my* dream."

Let me point again to the man Joseph. I'm sure when Joseph was trapped in that pit, waiting until his brothers sold him as a slave, he said to himself, *My Lord God, what is happening? This isn't the way the dream is supposed to come out. This is not the way I dreamed it!*

I'm sure that later, when Joseph found himself working as a servant in Egypt, he had many opportunitites to say, "Wait a minute, God. You're making a mistake! Here I am a *servant,* but I'm supposed to be a *leader.* I'm supposed to become the one everybody bows down to!"

And I know when Joseph was thrown into prison on false charges, his dream was shattered. But he kept believing God. He could not understand *how* it could be, but he remained true to the Lord God Jehovah, even though he was a prisoner in a foreign land.

Joseph's dream became very obscure in that Egyptian dungeon. Bible historians believe more than a decade passed before it became a reality.

But about 13 years after he entered Egypt as a slave, Joseph stood in Egypt as prime minister, controlling storehouses God had warned him to stock with food.

His brothers bowed before him. They didn't know who he was. They were hungry, for there was famine in their land.

It happened just like God gave it to Joseph — but it wasn't easy. At any point during those years, Joseph could have decided to quit, and the dream would have gone down with him. God would have had to look around for somebody else to fulfill what He wanted done.

God has given many people dreams and visions to accomplish for Him. The sad part is that many have quit when they reached a hard part, and their shattered dream was laid on a shelf to collect dust.

Has God had to go out and look for somebody to do *your* job? Maybe He had to use someone who didn't have all your qualifications, but when He asked you, you refused. They had a willing heart, and they pressed forward with that dream until it became a reality and souls were snatched from the burning pits of hell.

Chapter 2
God Gave Me a Dream

I know the dream God can give you. I know that the enemy can make that dream become so blurry that it's almost obscured at times from your spiritual sight.

Many years ago God gave me a dream when I was an 18-year-old student at Southwestern Assembly of God College in Waxahachie, Texas. As I knelt praying one night in my room, I saw myself preaching to huge crowds of all races. I'm 41 now, but I never forgot that dream.

For a while I took a church and was going to be pastor. Then one day I realized I'd laid that dream on the shelf, and I had to get it out, dust it off, and put it back down in my spirit and begin to do what God wanted me to do.

If I had stayed at that church (I was then associate pastor), it would have been mine. It was all set. But that wasn't God's plan. He had to remind me of my dream. I had to get hold of it and go with it again.

God gave me a dream to go around this world and preach the Gospel of the Lord Jesus Christ. I've been in Africa, I'm going to the Philippines. I want to go to England, where churches are closing by the hundreds. I want to go to the uttermost parts of the world to minister.

I've had a vision, too, of building overseas centers to teach native workers. The day of the white missionary's going in and doing everything is over. He can go in, however, and teach national workers to do the job.

We don't bring national workers to RHEMA Bible Training Center in Tulsa. If they come to North America, they get westernized. They don't want to return to villages where they don't have electricity, running water, radio, television, and other modern conveniences. But if we can take the school to them and train them in their homelands, they can go out and train others — and they can begin to believe God to have modern conveniences.

They can learn to turn impossible situations into possibilities because of the power of God!

As I told Brother T. L. Osborn the other day, I know I could go to Africa and hold big crusades, but I really don't care about that. I enjoy going into the villages and ministering personally to the 200 or 300 who come out. It is exciting.

I've ridden for hours in a van on little more than a cow path to reach a village on the shores of Lake Victoria in Kenya. There I was greeted by an old, wrinkled, gray-haired native. He bowed and said, "Welcome, welcome. Thank you for coming. You are the first white man from any Protestant denomination who ever came to our village to preach about Jesus."

In one Kenyan village I preached, "If this faith message only works in America, then it's not the Word of God."

I told the villagers if they would believe God, God would give them crops. I told them if they would believe God, they could get a bicycle. Getting a bicycle to some of them is like our getting a fine car. I told them if they would believe God, they could have tin roofs on their houses instead of thatched roofs.

One year later I returned to that village for a pastors' conference. One man said, "Look here! Look here! God gave me a bicycle. I had the biggest sugar cane crop of anybody in the village; everybody else had a crop failure. I sold my crop and was able to buy a bicycle and a tin roof for my house. I was the only man in the village who had any prosperity at all out of his crop this year."

I have a dream and a vision to take people from RHEMA Bible Training Center, go around this world, and establish churches where people will preach the truth of the Word of God to these people.

During the past five years, if I hadn't known what God had told me to do in building RHEMA Bible Training Center — if I hadn't had the dream and vision of it — and if I hadn't dared to believe what God had told me — it would have been easy to quit. Many, many times the dream faded under the enemy's attacks.

You're going to have to get out your dream, dust it off, and begin to do what God has told you to do. You're going to have to continue to work harder, because the time is short. But if you'll believe God and do what God has asked you to do, it shall be accomplished.

Chapter 3
Dare To Believe
Your Dream

Dare to believe *your* dream. When it seems the devil has shattered that dream that came to you from God Himself, reach down, pick up those shattered pieces, put the dream back together, and continue to drive for success.

A dream becomes a reality because somebody wants it to be. It becomes a reality because somebody dares to dream a dream. They dare to believe in that dream. And they set out to make that dream become a reality.

We don't have electric lights today just because a man was walking along and stubbed his toe. No, we have electricity because a man said one day, "Electricity is real. It's a real substance. I believe I can harness it for the use of mankind." He set out to do the job, and he invented the electric light bulb.

In the process, his dream was destroyed hundreds of times. Every time Thomas A. Edison would start to give up, out of the depths and resources of his inner being something would say, "There is a substance — there is a material — that can take electricity and give it illumination, and it will benefit mankind."

Edison did not let go of his dream no matter how many times it shattered. Because he kept dreaming that dream, you and I today enjoy the advantages of the electric light bulb. Thomas A. Edison had dreamed a dream.

A famous Olympic athlete was another man who dreamed a dream and wouldn't let it go.

In the 1968 Olympics in Mexico City, a young American runner came off the last corner of the last event in the decathlon championship — and as the television cameras zeroed in on him, I could almost feel the agony etched in his face.

Bill Toomey had overcome every kind of adversity to get to that point. He had long dreamed of winning the decathlon, which consists of 10 track and field events divided into a two-day period.

For this last event, he had to run in cold rain in Mexico City's high altitude. (Anyone who knows anything about track and field knows that the worst possible time to run is on cold, wet days, because the muscles don't get warmed up sufficiently. They tear, pull, and cramp. I've been there. I know what I'm talking about.)

On this final day of the decathlon, Bill Toomey already had participated in nine of the ten most grueling events in the Olympics games. He said, "I haven't come this far to quit now."

As he lined up for the one-mile race, his body was saying, "You can't do it! You can't run anymore! You've had it!"

But 'way back in the inner resources of his mind was the dream he had dreamed for years and years: winning the decathlon. And when the starter cracked the gun, Bill Toomey took off running. One lap. Two laps. Three laps. Then he was finishing the race.

I know what he was feeling as he came off that last corner, headed for the home stretch. I know what it's like to feel every muscle in your body scream, "You can't force me anymore! I can't go on anymore!" I know what it's like to feel your lungs burn from lack of oxygen, but you press on, because you have a dream of winning.

When the TV cameras zeroed in, I could see the agony in every muscle in his body as he was coming down that last hundred or so yards toward the final tape. His muscles began to tense. I could see it in his face. I could see it in the flailing of his arms — but he kept his eyes fastened on the finish line.

I could see him begin to go a little faster, even though his physical body was screaming, "Quit, man! You don't have anything left!"

But there was something on the inside of him — a dream that had lived there for years — that kept telling him, "You can't quit now. You've practiced long. You've run too many miles."

He reached back and got the last bit of energy he had. I could see that drive as it began to pump adrenalin through his body. He exploded across the finish line.

Why? Because he had had a dream, and it was still down on the inside of him, and he would not let anything steal that dream from him.

Bill Toomey graced the winner's stand, and they placed the decathlon gold medal around his neck. His perseverance had made his dream come true!

Chapter 4
13 Boys with a Vision

I've been interested in track and field since my school days. I frequently give examples from track and field in my preaching, because I see so many similarities between this sport and the Christian walk.

Track and field is an individual sport, yet, at the same time, it's a team effort. The individual is competing for himself as well as for his team. Similarly, operating in the Body of Christ is an individual effort, yet it's also a team effort.

From the time I was in grade school just running around the block and running races with every kid in town, I dreamed of running in a regular race.

My cousin who lived with us dated a boy who ran track at a junior college. I used to watch him practice, and sometimes I even ran with him. This intensified my dream of running a race one day.

That dream became obliterated many times.

In my junior year in high school I went to a Christian boarding school so my mom could travel in the ministry with my dad. I discovered they had no track team at that school, and they never had had a track team at that school. My dream was gone.

I started talking it over with some of the other boys. I suggested, "Let's have a track team."

"Aw, Hagin, we can't have a track team."

I forgot that guy and went to somebody else. "Let's have a track team."

This guy said, "I always wanted to run track."

I went to another. He said, "I used to run track before I came to boarding school. Yes, I'm interested." My dream began to get a little brighter.

We asked the basketball coach. He said, "I don't know anything about track. I don't have time. I have other things to do."

I asked, "May we use the jerseys the basketball team wore?"

He said, "Yes, you may use those jerseys."

We got our history teacher to be our coach. He liked sports.

We bought our own shoes and running shorts.

I'll never forget that pitiful assemblage of 13 boys and one history teacher who went onto the field at the first track meet of the season. We looked like a circus, because we hadn't all bought the same kind of running shorts. Our jerseys were blue and gold. Some boys had red shorts on. You can imagine what blue and gold looked like with red. It didn't look too good.

All the other teams had their warm-up suits on. Some of us had old sweat suits. Others wore jeans. A few had their own sweat shirts. One boy had Mickey Mouse on the front of his.

Can you imagine this bunch out on the field with all the other schools' teams in their classy uniforms?

We started practicing for the 880 relay. We were going to practice our relay hand-offs. Everybody else had those nice, hollow batons. We came out on the field passing a broomstick back and forth. That's all we had.

I had taken the broom from my dormitory room, gone down to the shop, borrowed a saw, measured the broom, and sawed it off. That's where we got our relay baton. For the rest of the school year I had to sweep my room out with a short-handled broom.

But, you see, the 13 of us had a dream. We dreamed of running. We wanted a team. At first our dream was just of running a race. We went out and ran. We started taking first places — we started winning!

Soon they quit laughing at the bunch of clowns and the history teacher, because the bunch of clowns and the history teacher were beating everybody. Then they started saying, "Where did this bunch come from?"

We realized we had more than we thought. Our dream increased. We dreamed of running in the state track meet.

Everybody knows that a team with neither an experienced coach nor proper equipment doesn't make the state track meet — that just wouldn't happen. But 7 out of our 13-man track team went to the state track meet in May 1957. The newspaper called us "The Cinderella Seven."

Our dream was fulfilled the night of May 18, 1957. The starting gun cracked at 9 o'clock sharp. One minute and 37 seconds later, the 880 relay was over. I will never forget it as long as I live.

I'll never forget how I began to see white spots in front of my eyes 20 yards from the fellow I was to hand the baton off to. My lungs were burning inside of me for lack of oxygen. My legs felt like rubber.

But somewhere down on the inside of me was a dream: a dream of winning. And when those white spots began to appear, an incident from the past came back to my mind. The 880 relay faded . . . I went back to the only day my dad had ever been able to be present to see me compete in a track meet.

I imagined I was coming off that curve, churning with everything I had, when down by the finish line I saw my dad reach out, and I heard him holler, "Come on, boy! Come on, boy! Come on, boy! Come on, boy!"

His words began to ring in my ears: "Come on, boy! Come on, boy! Run, Slim! Run, Slim . . . ."

I reached back, got strength from somewhere deep within, and finished. Our team won the meet that day!

I want to say something to all who have picked up the baton to run in the race for our Lord Jesus Christ but your dream has been obliterated by circumstances: *The finish line is just a little further ahead!*

You're in the championship game of life right now. The devil is doing everything he can to steal your dreams from you, but now is the time for you to stand and dream your dreams and visions — and help bring the King of Kings and Lord of Lords back to earth. We'll reign with Him forevermore.

I can see Jesus Christ leaning out across the finish line hollering, "Come on, man! Come on, woman! Just a few more steps and you've got it made! Don't lose the dream now! Run to victory! Run to victory!"

Chapter 5
The Church's Vision:
The World

Many say, "Oh, wouldn't it have been wonderful to have lived in the days of Jesus and the disciples? Wouldn't it have been wonderful to have watched Jesus ascend into heaven?"

I disagree. *This* is the greatest hour there ever was, because *this* is the day and hour we're going to see Jesus come back. *This* is the greatest hour in history! I'm excited about working for Jesus.

God is giving dreams and visions to pastors and others all over the world. We in the charismatic movement must realize that God is giving people these dreams and visions for one purpose only: to snatch mankind from the hands of the enemy — from the very fires of hell itself!

Millions and millions of people are chained with the chains of sin — sickness, poverty, disease — yet all we charismatics do is talk about believing for another expensive car, house, etc.

This faith message we preach is not a get-rich-quick scheme. I believe in prosperity as much as anyone else, and I believe the Word of God teaches it, but the Church of the Lord Jesus Christ does not exist for you to live in fine houses, wear fine clothes, and drive fine automobiles. The Church of the Lord Jesus Christ exists for the salvation of men's souls. The main message is Jesus Christ and Him crucified.

All of these other things, such as prosperity, are fringe

benefits of the Word and power of God. Do you want to know how to have all of these benefits? Get out and start winning souls. Set people free from the devil's bondage. You'll find you can't keep success from falling on you. God will see to it if you'll take care of His business first.

Thank God for our good homes and so forth, but I wonder how many of us would still be willing to follow Jesus if we didn't have all the prosperity we now enjoy? (That will tell you how sold out you are to God.)

I realize some people have taken the things we preach and have perverted them. However, if they would listen to what Brother Hagin has to say, they would discover that the first thing any born-again, Spirit-filled Christian should be involved with is a vision for a lost and dying world.

I have a vision of the world. I have dreamed a dream of the world. I have traveled in it. I have preached in those mud huts and brush arbors in Africa. I love those people. They need God.

My heart cries within me when I think of all the preachers and teachers who are sitting around doing nothing.

My heart cries within me when I think of the teeming millions around the world who have heard about Jesus and have accepted Him in some big crusade, yet they've never been able to mature spiritually, because nobody has taught them the power of faith in God.

I asked a man the other day, "Did God call you to minister?"

"Yes," he replied.

"Then why don't you get out and get into the ministry?"

"Oh, I don't know if I could make enough money," he said.

I said, "That's part of your problem. You don't believe in God, because if you believed God called you, and if you believed in yourself, you'd be out there doing something about it instead of sitting here, waiting for somebody to hand you something on a silver platter."

In God's work, as in anything else, you don't get something for nothing.

"You're not preaching faith now," somebody will complain.

Yes, I am. You don't get something for nothing. You've got to have faith before you get anything. *You spend something to receive: You spend your faith.* And faith cometh by hearing, and hearing by the Word of God.

Our problem is that we dream the dream one minute and want it to be manifested the next. It doesn't happen that way, either in the spiritual or the natural worlds.

When a man has a dream for a big shopping center, an apartment complex, etc., he doesn't sit in his office with his architect one day and expect to see the finished complex the next. Sometimes the project will be built in phases. It may be years before it's completed.

Chapter 6
A Word to Ministers

I believe God is raising up mighty churches around the world that will preach the truth of the Gospel of the Lord Jesus Christ — the *real* faith message.

God has given some of you pastors a dream for a church and other buildings, yet when you look out the window, all you see is the bare ground you've bought to build on, or perhaps you've started by building one room. But the dream is real, even though it's not happening as fast as you want it to.

You've got to continue to see the dream or vision God gave you with the eye of faith. It's got to be real to you. You must see your dream in its completed form, even though the devil is harassing you.

Every time you take a step, it seems he digs the foundation out from under your feet, and you slip. Your dream loses its inspiration and reality. Finally it dies, lying dormant deep within your spirit.

You may feel that way right now: trapped, distressed, an utter failure. But you must not look at your present circumstances; you must begin to believe God and the dream He gave you.

Whenever your circumstances say, "There is no way this can happen," you must dare to dream big! You must realize that God has placed you where you're at at this particular time in your life. And He put you there for success, not failure!

Some of you have a dream of a traveling ministry. Others have a dream of pastoring. That dream has to live big inside of you. That dream must ring true within your soul, despite all that the devil is throwing at you.

Through it all, you must look through the haze of circumstances and see the finish line down the road.

A man running a natural race has only the natural, soulish part of man to draw from. You who are running a spiritual race also have the spirit part of man. Therefore, you can reach into your spirit, push through the last 50 yards to victory, and make the dream God gave you come true.

No, it won't be easy. But you've got to dare to believe what God told you. It doesn't matter whether anybody else believes it or not; *you've* got to believe what God says to you. God gave you that vision. Don't quit now.

It may look like it's hopeless. But if you'll listen to your spirit down on the inside of you, that spirit is saying, "You can't quit now! *There's the victory just over the hill!*"

You see, God by His Spirit is leading you and me. He's showing us the way to success. But many of us don't like the road to success our dream has taken us on. It's not paved with the soft cushions and the silver lining we thought it would be paved with. Our dream is not being accomplished with the ease with which we thought it should be accomplished.

When God called you into the ministry and gave you a dream of that ministry, He never told you it would be easy. Nowhere in the Word did He ever say it would be easy. But He did say in Mark 9:23, *"all things are possible to him that believeth."*

Keep believing in the dream. Let it manifest by phases as God gives it to you. You'll see the reality of it eventually. Don't be discouraged because it's not happening quickly. Grab hold of the dream God gave you and never let it go!

When God gives you a dream to carry out, you can walk up to the devil's territory, if he's holding onto it, and say, "In the Name of the Lord Jesus Christ, this is where my dream is supposed to be. You devil, get out of here right now!"

Then you plant yourself there, saying, "In the Name of Jesus, I can do all things through Him. I will build what God has given me to build on this spot, and neither the enemy nor anybody else will take it away from me!"

Or you can have a pity party, pat yourself on the back, and say, "Well, I'm nothing."

I'm tired of hearing that so-called religious jargon that we're tired and lonely; we're the meekest and the lowliest; "Here we wander like a beggar, through the heat and cold . . . ."

Believe in God! Believe in yourself! There never was a person who succeeded in life who didn't believe he could do it. A farmer must believe he can grow crops before he'll ever grow any. Otherwise, he would never go out and till the soil and plant the seeds. And you're certainly not going to harvest anything unless you plant it.

Dare to believe what God has said in His Word. Dare to believe in yourself. You've got to dare to believe your dream is from God. You've got to dare to believe in yourself — that you can accomplish it through Jesus Christ who lives inside you.

You may argue, "But I don't want to be egotistical. I don't want to be stuck up." That's a lie the devil has concocted to cause people not to succeed. Somebody's always talking about being humble. There are some people who are so humble they are proud of their humility!

Religious people will tell you, "Don't get conceited. You can't have people looking up to you. You've always got to lift up Jesus." We know that — we all know that — but the devil tries to rob people through false modesty, too.

When someone tells them, "That was a great sermon," or "You did a wonderful job building this church," they say, "Oh, that's nothing. I'm nothing. It's just the Lord."

God can't do anything on this earth without a man or a woman who will do it for Him. Yes, we *know* God is behind it all, but God has so ordained it that He would work through mankind. It's God's plan of action; therefore, we need to begin to believe in ourselves. We need to read Philippians 4:13, *"I can do all things through Christ which strengtheneth me."* Notice it says *"I* can."

In Acts 4, we find Peter and John walking by the gate called Beautiful. Peter wasn't suffering from false modesty when he looked down at the crippled beggar and said, "I don't have any silver or gold in my pockets, BUT LOOK ON US!"

People want to preach about everything else in this passage of Scripture. They want to preach about the man who was healed. They want to preach that Peter was a pauper. (It so happened that he didn't have any money at that particular time, but that's not enough to build a doctrine on!) They want to preach, "We're not supposed to have anything." They're missing the point.

They never want to preach that Peter looked at the beggar and said "Hey! If you want something, LOOK ON US! We've got something!"

When Peter said that, he knew he had the power of God inside him. It wasn't Peter's faith that beggar saw. All of a sudden the beggar began to see the hand of Jesus and the faith of Jesus Christ reaching down to him, because the power of God inside Peter came out to him.

You need to dare to believe in yourself the way Peter did. That is different from being conceited.

I don't believe there is anything I can't do. Why? Because God saved me by the blood of the Lord Jesus Christ His Son, and He gives me my strength. Therefore, I can do all things through Christ who strengthens me. ALL things!

We who are in the ministry need to get the idea across to believers that they are somebody. They are children of God. And they have the right and privilege of walking through this earth using the Name of the Lord Jesus Christ as their power of attorney.

Chapter 7
Quit Comparing

You ministers need to quit comparing yourself with some other minister and his church.

Not everybody's church will run 2,000 people — but thank God for those that will. Thousands of you pastors are doing the job God called you to with 200, 100, or even 50 or 25 people.

Compare yourself with what God told you to do. If it measures up, then you can see Jesus saying to you, "Stay in there! Keep running the race! You've got it made!"

I do believe God has spoken to certain people to establish large regional churches across the continent. We can already see them beginning to dot the United States.

We've got one on the West Coast with Fred Price's church. We've got another in Houston with John Osteen's. These men dreamed a dream. They never thought their churches would be that big; they started small. They did what God told them to do.

But even though these large regional churches are beginning to develop across the country, it's not for you to try to measure your church and your success by them. Measure your dream with the vision God has placed within your heart. Then run your race to victory until we all get home.

In this race there doesn't have to be any second place. All of us can stand on the winner's stand at the Judgment Seat of Christ and receive the crown as Jesus says, "Well done, good and faithful servant. You have run the race with patience. Now enter into rest, and let's have a good victory party."

I want to encourage you that your dream is still real. Begin to brush the dust and cobwebs away from it. Quit comparing your dream with someone else's. Compare your dream with what God said to you.

Dare to believe in the dream God gave you. Dare to believe in it even though it becomes destroyed.

Don't throw it away. Even though it becomes obscure, don't leave it.

Believe in yourself. Believe in what God said for you to do.

Take the impossible and turn it into the possible for God this day. The time for victory in your life is *now!*

Dream your dream and make it become a reality, because God in His Word has said so.

Prophecy

Don't give up. Don't give up.
Put that dream back together.
Put it back together,
and do what you know to do,
and it will come out all right.

Don't lay it down.
If you lay it down,
I don't have anybody else to pick it up,
saith the Lord.

You've got to do the job.
I gave it to you to do.
Don't transfer it to somebody else.
You do it.

Many have I called.
Many have I spoken to.
Many have I showed the dream,
but they have rejected;
they have turned Me aside.

To you I have given
what they would not take.
To you I have given
because you said,
"Lord, here am I; send me."

When others turned aside
because it wasn't big enough.
When others said,
"Lord, I want the big ministry,"
You did what I told you to do.

Relax in Me, and quit comparing yourself
with your fellow ministers and your peers.
Quit comparing your ministry
with their ministry.

Compare your ministry
with what I told you to do,
and you'll rejoice,
because you'll see that it already has surpassed
what I told you to do,
and you have gone on to a bigger dream.
You have advanced to another dream.

Keep moving with My Spirit,
and I will show you
the greatest victory of all.